DANCING BLUES

ARKS

MARY SHEEPSHANKS

Fighting Cock Press

Published by Fighting Cock Press 2004

Fighting Cock Press

Fighting Cock Press:
45 Middlethorpe Drive
York
YO24 1NA

Editor: Pauline Kirk
Consultant: Mabel Ferrett

Printed by Peepal Tree Press
Cover Design by Graham Rust
Original Fighting Cock Logo by Stanley Chapman

ISBN 0 906744 27 X

Acknowledgements are due to the following:

Journals
Acumen, Aireings, Camphill Correspondence, The Countryman, Envoi, Farmers Weekly, The Field, Gabriel, The Lady, Orbis, Other Poetry, Pennine Platform, Second Light, The Spectator, Yorkshire Journal

Anthologies
Windfall edited by Alison Chisholm and Peggy Poole
Perceptions edited by Peggy Poole
Webbed Skylights of Tall Oaks edited by Clare Chapman

Also by Mary Sheepshanks

Fiction
A Price for Everything
Facing the Music
Picking up the Pieces
Off-Balance
The Venetian House (writing as Mary Nickson)

Non Fiction
The Bird of my Loving
(*A personal response to loss and grief*)

Poetry
Patterns in the Dark
Thinning Grapes
Kingfisher Days

For Robin and Lilias

with love

Contents

Unexpected Passenger

Classic FM spills memories in my car.
As I drive northwards on the motorway
landmarks fly past with disconcerting speed
– but I travel backwards: hear again

the muffled boom of bells beneath the sea
a swish of censers swinging through the waves
the chant of salt-corroded psalms
and plainsong drowned by the swell of the tide.

You play Debussy on the Steinway
before dinner and notes float up the stairs
to summon me from the end
of the dark passage where silence is my enemy.

I flit in my white night-dress
to sit illicitly on the top step,
caught in a spell of sound, while you conjure
caverns and shells and a lost congregation.

Now, as the prelude fades,
your presence lingers and I recall
the tolling of another bell on a Welsh hillside
– feel again the airtight disapproval

of the grown-ups at your way of life
and all those talents scattered
with such prodigality, but… I thank you
for the music that you gave a child.

Storm ...
...on Pockstones Moor

When earth is laced to sky by silver threads
and rocks turn black and rivers overflow,
reckless, the swallows windsurf on the gale
but bracken, suppliant, kneels before its blow.

White-lipped with panic, frantic moorland streams
scramble to jump the queue and reach the sea;
timpanist winds hurl music through the air
and trees conduct a passionate symphony.

Migration

High on my windswept hill
I live beneath a flight path.

Each year I thrill
to hear the whispering wings
and haunting fog-horn cry
before I see ship's anchors tossed
across the ripples of an ocean sky.

Strong pinions beat and stretch
to shift the air and race
the striptease act of autumn trees;

their rhythmic music sings
of hedgerow berries' juicy yield
and hawthorn skies at dusk;
first frosts on stubble fields,
a search for winter food;
flick-knives concealed
inside the pockets of
a gangster breeze.

Evenings grow dark again
and summer's dead

– but
        the wild geese are back
and sailing overhead.

Making Summer Pudding

Crouched on an upturned bucket, fingers stained,
I weigh the rival claims of summer fruit:
blackcurrants smell of old tom cat, but gleam
glossy as toe-caps on a soldier's boot;

delicious on their own, their forceful zest
can dominate a mix, and sometimes wreck
the subtle character of milder tastes
– would-be dictators must be kept in check.

Raspberries and redcurrants, paired in heaven,
– the Romeos and Juliets of the punnet –
possess ingredients for a perfect marriage
like rhyme and meter joining in a sonnet.

Strawberries, for me, are sovereigns of the clan:
snow-capped with sugar, avalanched in cream,
or gorged in secret underneath the net –
forbidden fruit of all our childhood dreams.

I'll blend my fruit together in a pan,
spoon it in bread-lined bowls and pack down tight;
add weights – heavy as age – to draw the juice
and hope for once I get life's balance right!

After the Flood

While gloomy heifers squelch
hock-deep in mud,
and loops of water
fishscale down my lane
the river, furtive as a guilty dog,
slinks back to bed again.

I dry the carpets out
and think of Mrs Noah
– unsung heroine of another flood.

After the Ark had landed
on the mountain top,
no doubt she was the one to wield the mop
while Noah, plumped by prophesy,
gave out advice.

And what about those teenage sons
with silly names?
Did they slick down their hair
with *Slime-of-Ararat,*
and skive behind the hippo sheds
to roll a joint of olive leaves
– then disappear while she cleared up?

Once the flood was over,
did she suffer a reaction
to cramped days of stress
(like families at Christmas time)
and long to get the crisis spirit back
without the mess?

But I bet she just got on with it
– and let her smug old Noah
snaffle all the praise.

Unseasonable Songs

The sun gives unexpected gifts today
beguiling birds to unwrap summer songs
and carol thoughts of icicles away.
Do they not realise it is Christmas time?
Have seasons' calculations gone so wrong?

Trees dip their finest nibs in Indian ink
to sketch bare branches on December sky,
but listening to these choristers you'd think
they had forgotten last week's fog and rime
and set their instincts' thermostat awry.

Though bonfire feathers presage colder flights,
thrushes hang *Jubilates* from each perch
and thread green alleluias through the light
– less like a scene for Winter's pantomime
than Easter decorations round a church.

Goldcrests

I peer through keyholes in the conifers,
eavesdrop on confidential pillow-talk
among the pines
to catch a glimpse of
pinpoint golden lights
winking and flickering
through disguising green.

Discreet in combat camouflage
they're hard to see
searching for spiders
in September trees,
but mini miners' lamps
strapped on to tiny heads
give them away;
their beaks are pickaxe sharp,
top notes so high
I'm lucky still to hear
their treble pipe:
"cedar-cedar-cedar-scissor-tree"
– a warning cry.

I am the paparazzi come to spy
With telescopic lens upon their privacy.
I would not like the same thing
done to me.

Merlin

Once – a pirate on the high winds –
it feathered oars to row rough rivers of sky
and set off siren screams to panic prey;
skimmed over hill and heather to wield
a lethal knife on mouse and meadow pipit,
then offered headless corpses to its mate
– small gangster of the plucking-post,

Today, a terrorist's last traces seep
into peaty soil to nourish future plants;
bleached bones, brittle as heartbreak,
lie scattered by a dry-stone wall and a skull
– disturbing as Venetian masks at Carnival –
has metamorphosed as a harmless nib
to scratch an epitaph on moorland grass.

A Mouthful of Pins

She used to stand me on a table
– turning me round and round –
like a chicken on a spit –
and spoke with tucked-in lips
sieving her words to a puree
through a mouthful of pins.

She was hard to understand
as she mumbled to my mother
about letting-out or taking-in,
buttons versus zips
on something mysterious
called *The Waistband.*

She kept a tin of mints and buttons,
chalk and hooks-and-eyes.
I dreamed of shop-bought dresses
but swivelled round – obedient –
as she tacked me into hand-me-downs
to alter them for size.

Now as I try on writing styles
but search for my own voice
I still seem stuck with 'second-hand'
and I wish she'd come again
with her mouthful of pins
to make a tailor-made one

just for me... that really fits.

Looking for Lines

A drift of butterflies,
– filigree flakes of snow –
hover above dark ivy
over my garden wall,
searching for nectar.

Advance, retreat, advance:
in triple or quadruple time
they pirouette and polka,
testing uncertainties
– trying new dances.

Are they the unwritten words
– tentative but persistent –
which flutter in my head
hunting hopefully
for lines to land on?

If I hold my breath
perhaps onr may pause…
…settle on a leaf
and metamorphose
into verse?

Best Foot Forward

For Susannah – who saw the advertisement

Limpety-hopody off to chiropody,
after a treatment they skateboard outside
in exercise sandals – from vicars to vandals
Miss Skidmore's patients gratefully glide.

With no more verrucas men get out of snookers
and slide round the table to pocket the pink;
chaps without bunions will soon leave their onions
to rot on allotments, and make for the rink.

Princes from palaces walk without calluses
tramps with no foot-rot parade down the street
arthritic old dancers form sets of "The Lancers"
for Miss Skidmore's patients are light on their feet.

Retired from the army one soldier went barmy,
(his feet were so painful he laid down his arms)
his reason was slipping till she started clipping
but now the brave hero's been saved by her charms.

When digits are corny she makes him feel horny
– as she plasters a toe dare he call her "My Sweet"?
Her Romeo marches on flat fallen arches
but *Skidmore Deodorant*'s working a treat.

"Oh lovely Miss Skidmore, I do wish you did more!
Let's slip off together, I simply can't wait
to trip the fantastic in leather or plastic
and walk in your footsteps and be your sole-mate."

Skipety-jumpety, bride far from frumpety
bridegroom now walking as though upon air:
Off to the church they dash, newspaper headline splash:
"SKIDMORE WEDS FOOT-GUARD – SALUTE HAPPY PAIR"

A Jaundiced View?

"How one dreads April for the daffodils,"
says the jowled gentleman of lofty mien
with whom I have the privilege to dine
on duck breasts (rare) and vintage Bordeaux (fine).

"It makes me ill when I encounter yellow
allowed to spread like litter down our roads -
don't you agree that fines should be imposed
on those who won't keep daffodils enclosed?

Snowdrops in February I can just digest
and hellebores don't cause too much collapse.
Narcissi on a pale March day ?... perhaps...
but those gold trumpets are a gruesome lapse

of taste. A-h-h crème brûlée! A spoonful more
and the meringue with chocolat caraque.
You can't be serious! Don't say you *like*
such brash vulgarity upon a stalk!"

His shocked revulsion gives me food for thought
the simple view of Spring's been scoffed away:
my fence keeps dogs inside and deer at bay,
but... how do I know my daffodils won't stray?

Midsummer Song

Is there midsummer madness this Midsummer's Eve?
There's magic in plenty for those who believe
that dreams can take wing like the swallows and fly
where bluebells meander by oceans of sky.

Shall we go exploring on Midsummer Day
where hedgerows of hawthorn white-water their way
down rafts by the river while skylarks trapeze
– dizzily carolling over the trees.

What midsummer madness for Midsummer Night?
I may be past passion – but not past delight
if the sun lays a lover-like touch on my back
or the moon sketches silverpoint runes on my track.

June's magical days cast a spell as they pass
light as midsummer breezes which feather the grass
so with words as my music, for you I will play
a medley of midsummer madness today.

The Lie of the Grass

Love is like
the strongest wind
the softest breeze
which in their passing
leave memories
in the lie of the grass.

So may the imprint
of your love
stay on the meadow
of my life

for ever.

Vision

He stares at his mother
through blacked-out windows
but unfurls in sunshine
as she smiles at him
with her voice.

He maps her face
with fingertips;
learns the light and shade of her
by touch; memorises
her likeness in his hands.

I watch and cannot
share his private image
– but who can say whether
I perceive such beauty
through my eyes?

November Walk

What did the two dogs see
which made them jam on all the brakes
so suddenly?

Why did they growl and bristle,
dip their tails and tremble
on the muddy track –
then skirt, reluctantly, a presence
not perceived by me?

We've tramped this route
for years, to post my letters,
in the scarlet box
fixed to the old stone wall.

It's usually a joyful walk
of expectations, then release,
with fruitless squirrel-chases
through the woods;
the scent of hares;
a roe-deer drinking in the stream;
wings in the wind
and messages round trees.

But on this poppy-red
November morning,
with shepherds' warnings
painted on the sky,
my dogs experienced
something strange upon our way.

Could they have known it was
Remembrance Day?

Something Indefinable

(Le Vieillard et son Petit-Fils)

A glimpse through the window
of water and trees: one vertical rock
emerging, shark-like, from the sea;
a track, which snakes its story
round the far side of a hill.

The foreground colour's strong:
man's robe, child's cap – a flame of red;
their features clear as focussed photographs
(we'd know this couple if we met them in the street)
and yet this portrait's gift does not lie in a likeness.

The grandson sees beyond
distorted, warty nose, sparse hair, slack skin –
perceiving only warmth and humour
as he rests open palms upon the old man's sleeve,
returning look for look with confidence.

Was it through techniques
learnt in long apprenticeship or by the Grace of God
that Ghirlandaio wove this potent spell –
could see before him something indefinable
...then conjure it on canvas from a pot of paint?

Canute

Once I dashed
towards the sea
to surf the breakers,
relishing the rush
of the ocean's thrilling dance:
participating - laughing.

Now I narrow my eyes
at the horizon
and consider the forecast.

I hope to savour
the treasury of shells
I have collected
with such pleasure
– even gather new ones –
before winter's high rollers,
sweep me to an unknown destination,
but as the waves approach
I wonder:

when that riptide comes…
……can I go willingly ?

Last Visit

"She may not recognise you dear," the sister warns
although her face lights up at my approach.
"Did I know that you were coming?"
She is anxious and confused
– no safe familiar pegs to hang her memories on
in this strange world of trolleys, drips and hoists;
unyielding pillows and unfriendly bed.

"Time to take your analgesics, pet"
– small pills in plastic pot placed on a tray –
"just take this drink and try to swallow them."
"*Do* I have pain?" she asks with interest and surprise,
long years ago a specialist nurse herself.
"No dear – you're having PAINKILLERS instead."

The staff are kind but treat her like a child
– tidy extraneous dignity away:
"She's very deaf, you'll need to shout
at her," she hears one carer say.
I know, with shame, I could not do their job
yet am affronted all the same
at the assumption that with memory-loss
all understanding's gone astray.

"I'm sure I know you , darling – but who *are* you?"
Bewildered and afraid, she takes my hand,
drawing some comfort from the contact
but troubled by the black holes in her jigsaw
which she tries – but fails – to fill.
Where have they gone, those treacherous missing bits?

I take her on a retrospective trip
hoping to guide her footsteps – switch on lights:
"Do you remember when…"
I try to click my 'mouse' on the right option
to open up the folder of her life – to no avail.
"I'm lost," she tells me with despair. "Completely lost
– I don't know who I am or where I live…."

I look back as I leave the ward
and intercept her pleading, puzzled gaze:
my final memory of her – one I can't delete.

Willowherb

Widow's Lament keeps watch with grief
along the fallen beech tree's length
and mourns with rain-drop tears the loss
of sap-green leaves and silver strength.

This fallen giant, once so strong
it stood against the wildest storm,
has by the years been laid to rest
a silent, silken-shrouded form.

Under its vaulted nave of green,
once cowslips danced to summer's band;
against mid-winter's heartbreak sky
its steel-cold silhouette would stand.

Now rain drum-beats a sad farewell
bent bracken-stalks bewail a death
and through its broken branches sighs
the whisper of a dying breath.

(Rosebay Willowherb is known in Scotland as *The Widow's Lament* because it often grows beside fallen trees)

Lily of the Valley

The painting is sub-titled "Happiness Regained"
but I had not read the caption
when I chose the card
– an inadequate vehicle by which to send
love and support to the anguished friend,
who weeps or stares in psychiatric ward.

"Count your blessings. Think of the children.
You shouldn't feel like this at such a happy time.
How did you get yourself in such a state
– you who have everything to live for?"

Longing to want to live – guiltily hoping to end –
she is ashamed of her collapse:
advice brings no relief;
her self-reproaches are a dentist's drill
upon a screaming nerve.
The black void wheedles siren songs
that will not go away.

She floats just out of reach:
frantically waving on the shores of her despair
her family throw life-lines which she cannot catch;
weeds drag her limbs
and slime their creepy fingers in her ears;
the water laps too near her nostrils.

"Just take the pills – and wait" the doctors say.

In the post-card picture
tear-drops cling to one green leaf
but up above, small chiming bells climb ladders.
Will they – perhaps – ring hopes that she can hear
above the sucking slough of her despond?

Keeping to the Pavement

When the wind rides rough in a vagabond sky
I think of the wagon I failed to buy –
a gypsy wagon with dandelion wheels
and a rounded top as green as the hills;
strong shafts to harness a carefree steed
(a wall-eyed skewbald of Romany breed)
to clip-clop under the Milky Way
or travel on little-known roads by day.

I attended the auction but lost my nerve
so it went to a bidder with buccaneer verve.
I'd hoped it was mine, but mislaid my voice
and stepped on the pavement of coward's choice.
If I'd been bolder it could have been mine
but I watched it vanish – all dazzle and shine,
with curlicue scrolls painted blue and red –
as it rolled away with my dreams instead.

Spelling Olive

Oil

Green and black and liquid gold
old into new, new into old.

Life

Arrivals, departures – new growth provides
choices and chance where the trunk divides.

Ideas

Light threading silver through leaves and vines
longings cold-pressed into words and lines.

View

Visions, adventures, reality
challenge of mountains, daydreams of sea.

Exit

End or eternity? Which will it be
when I pass through the fork in my olive tree?

The Val D'Orcia

God, in a Van Gogh mood, has dipped a hand
in ochre dyes to rake long fingers through
the barley-stubble stretches of July,
depicting sweeps of gold in furrowed lines,
stitching the hemline of Madonna sky ;
thumbprints are pressed in whorls – as though to prove
he'd more designs in mind for Tuscany
than silver olive-groves, round hills and vines.

South of Pienza, see where he has stretched
this broader canvas on the countryside;
splashed exclamation marks of Cypress trees
to herringbone their shadows up the land;
mixed on the palette every saffron shade
of burnished straw, pale sand and yellowed greys:
tossing out challenges, inviting risks
– rocketing daydreams to infinity.

Postcard

A watercolour
turns a rusty key:

white house, blue paintwork
– bluer sky – stray cats;
a bougainvillea
lolling down one wall;
geraniums, stiff,
in terracotta pots:
and oh, you're there again,
…still there with me.

Kingfishers borrow
feathers from the waves;
a gasp of dolphins
arrows past our bay.
Cicadas beat out
rhythms to the heat
and, tireless, shake maracas
all the day.

Through star-long nights,
the scops owls call
as secrets rustle
in the olive leaves; then
when a pewter pathway
crosses moonlit sea
…I feel you there once more,
still there with me.

Gandalf the Grey – A Triumph for Twelfth Night
For Freddie Shirley, 6 January 2004

Gandalf the Grey – your past is a mystery:
nobody knows your pre-Shirley history.
Eyes lucent as lime-drops, fur coloured like smoke,
you were dressed "haute couture" in suiting "bespoke"
as you strolled up our drive, a cool cat, one June day
and soon made it clear you intended to stay.
Did you travel by broomstick, by lorry or car?
Did you hitchhike from Derby? Sail in on a star?
You seemed like an alien – a cat from above,
yet knew about humans, warm kitchens and love.
You weren't scared of Frenzy or Flurry or Ping
or the visiting dogs that relations *will* bring;
you exuded charisma, the word's now a platitude
a confident, nonchalant cat-with-an-attitude.
You captured our hearts and when we moved house
condescended to try an East Anglian mouse.

One night in December you sauntered outside
and did not return all that cold Christmastide.
Oh,Gandalf the Grey, cat-wizard of magic,
there followed adventures that might have been tragic:
for you went on a pub-crawl – you wicked old soak –
and for nearly a fortnight got stuck up an oak .
How did we find you? Did you cast a last spell?
We'll never be certain for wizards don't tell!
On the last stroke of midnight we heard on the air,
faint, feline and frantic, a cry of despair.
We set out with ladders and torches and rope
and hearts that were pounding with freshly-sparked hope
to rescued our stow-away cat from a tree,
dehydrated and starving – but living and free!
We shouted with triumph – a glad caterwaul –
and great is rejoicing at Ditchingham Hall!

The Python at the Party

For Belinda

A python came to the party
– an unlikely guest in Kensington.
James and Geordie and their friends
dressed in their birthday best
and having gorged on sausages and cake,
crammed in meringues and crisps
and asked for more,
went writhing with the python
on the floor.

"What did the python have for tea?"
a mother asked,
her voice a trifle tremulous and faint,
fearing her little daughter might become
a snakeskin bulge
of undigested morsel in reptilian tum.

The owner said, that unlike humans
pythons only eat when they are hungry
and it had been fed – three days before.
Such laudable restraint!

But what if the snake
should suffer from bulimia, and get
an overwhelming urge to stuff
even when it had really
had enough?

Could it be counted on,
this creature from the wild
to vomit back – intact –
a swallowed child?

The Snailephant
(*For Octavia – who first drew one for me*)

A snailephant is very large with tusks and tail and trunk
and should you meet a hungry one, you'd better do a bunk –
don't linger till it lumbers up with jaws all set to munch
for snailephants think little girls make quite a tasty lunch.

Unlike a slug, a snailephant can't slime along the ground,
but stumps around on huge grey legs and makes a thundering sound.
Most snailephants are musical and specially fond of humming
and this is most convenient as it warns you if one's coming.

A snailephant has rubber horns, which swivel on its head
and wears – because its shell is thin – a tartan rug in bed.
They often snack on sugar lumps, eat prickly shrubs like gorse;
and what d'you think they like to suck? Why peppermints of course!

If you can tame a snailephant, they make delightful pets
provided you keep two of them (for one alone will fret)
so hide some *Polos* in the trees, spread toothpaste on a crumpet
and play a lot of catchy tunes on xylophone or trumpet.

Then, if you see some snailephants come snuffling up your drive,
lasso a rope around their necks to capture them alive.
Next, tell them if they're very good and learn to wear a saddle,
you'll put your tricycle away and take them for a paddle,

for snailephants adore the wet and most of them are fond
of gambolling off to roll in bogs – or better still, a pond;
they're crazy keen on outdoor sport – a trunk's a useful racquet –
and if you throw a ball at them, you can be sure they'll whack it.

Most snailephants are prone to colds, so keep a special hanky,
for if yours gets a bunged-up trunk it might be cross and cranky.
Though normally quite timid beasts, it puts them in a rage
if people send them to the zoo or shut them in a cage.

They like to have their door ajar, if they are in a shed
and may well roar unless you put a nightlight by the bed;
don't read them scary books at night, or look at too much telly;
wash all their bedding once a week – it can get rather smelly.

When other children come to play and want, like you, to ride them
just warn them that your pet is wild and always stay beside them:
for *if you don't*, your snailephant, though it might sweetly greet them,
may wait until your back is turned, then seize your friends
– AND EAT THEM.

Daybreak

First, almost inaudible,
an orange whisper
rumours its approach
and then the sun looms up
so fast behind the hills
to switch on the machine
that daily churns
fresh sacks of fright and hope,
it's strange we do not feel
our wild world tilt and turn
before it sends us hurtling
willy-nilly down the slope.

Touching Wood

Just lightly touch a twig
from time to time
but never try to clutch
at a whole tree ……

…… for paper tigers
live in these you know,
and if they catch you
hanging on too much
they have a nasty tendency

to grow.

Return to Sender

Play my music for me:
you composed it
so my music is your music.

Show me the empty canvas
and help me choose the colours
– so my picture is your picture.

Be my choreographer:
and partner me in a pas de deux
– so your dance becomes our dance.

Be my paper and string:
wrap me in hope, bind me with courage
– but label me with your address
that in the end I may return to you.

For Huldine

11 August 2004

If death is but the first flight
of a fledgling bird – a test
for wings not so far fully tried –
then you'd already stretched yours out
for quite some time
to balance at the edge
of life's precarious nest
with laughter and high courage.

You turned your body's valiant fight,
into a springboard for your spirit's flight
– your song will always be
a song of joy.
You lit a flare of friendship
and we, who loved you much,
remain the richer for your life
and all the warmth and brightness
that you shared with us.

The Fall

I stand beneath a flowering tree:
its branches do not shelter me.
I walk among the rising wheat:
the blades are swords and cut my feet.
Unbearably beautiful the light
scorches the frailty of my sight.
The golden voices call my name:
I dare not answer them for shame.
One with these glories I would be
– or else from knowing them set free.

Echo

Impersonal upon some plan
a number might record the plot
in that far graveyard where you lie
– no headstone marks the spot.

Although time's plane has smoothed the scar
death's chisel carved so deep,
still, secretly, I speak your name
– hear your one cry in sleep.

You only breathed a single breath
to scorch my life with pain,
yet that breath started such a shout
its echoes still remain.

Hey Diddle Diddle

I fear the heebie-jeebies
– a tremulous disease
that afflicts my great Aunt Phoebe's
dipsomaniac Pekinese

When they get the screaming ab-dabs
(I've heard Aunt Phoebe say)
that the doctor gives them jab-jabs
to take the pain away.

Should they suffer from the willies
– a hyper-tensive state –
she gives the sillies pillies
with their biccies on a plate,

but when they get the jitters,
I've heard Aunt Phoebe tell
how she changes baby-sitters
and buys them fudge as well.

The jimjams bring on stasis
which makes their poor eyes bulge
– but what the cure for that is
I simply daren't divulge!

Armchair Travel

With a broomstick at the ready
you can travel through your ear,
flying off to magic places
steered by names you love to hear:

Piddletrenthide, Blubberhouses,
Patchewollock, Shangri-La;
frolic round the Isles of Scilly
spice your life in Zanzibar.

Yaks may yomp up Annapurna,
mermaids swim the Sound of Sleat –
Machu-Picchu must be mystic
Merthyr Tydfil might be sweet?

Mississippi sounds so sexy
Ballymoney bodes a spree…
Don't waste time on trains or airlines:
dreams are quicker – and they're free!

Working Out

I hate those women who work out
– their muscled, sanctimonious bums –
why must they always jog about
and boast of weight-loss to their chums?

I watch them as they swoop and rush
to thwack the ball round tennis courts
and bet they've all got raging thrush
inside their skintight lycra shorts.

I hate the way they go for runs –
why don't they stop to lean on gates,
dance blues to sky-larks, guzzle buns,
write sonnets, eat off cardboard plates?

I wish they'd read and laze and dream,
pick asphodel and bubble ballads –
instead of which they give up cream
and toy with cautious tuna salads.

If they would only binge on chips
– while scribbling plots of love or gore –
they might get bigger round the hips
but oh – I'd like them so much more!

In the Paradise Garden

(With compliments to The BBC and Sir David Attenborough)

Oh come my love and bounce for me
upon a leafy trampoline
and make the pliant branches swing,
then flaunt your iridescent dress
while ravished by my dowdiness.
Oh make the ground your circus ring
let all the forest hear you sing
and you shall be my lyre king
and I, in paradise, your queen.

Oh come my love and make for me
a jewelled house, a dancing byre,
filled up with gems for my delight;
trapeze for me above a chasm –
then give me just one swift orgasm.
My future will be far from bright
after that moment of delight:
a single mother, day and night
– while you sod off in bright attire!

Round Robins

Another round robin for Christmas, forsooth:
how exciting – the Borehams have potty-trained Ruth!
We worried all year, but are terribly happy
the prodigy child has dispensed with her nappy.

The Borehams went diving: this year, for a lark,
they gave dolphins a miss to swim with a shark.
Sharks also, they tell us, have healing potential –
Val lost a leg, but two legs aren't *essential.*

Now she hops for her college, her parents feel proud,
and her friends are supportive – a wonderful crowd
of committed young Christians, who constantly strive
to liven up Sundays with jingles and jive;

they kiss and they hug as they spread the Good News
– and the vicar is thrilled by new bums on his pews.
(It was sad that poor Valerie fell in the aisle
but she rose to her foot with a born-again smile).

Sandra has finished her final exams
– she was heading for A grades while still in her pram –
she now plays the panpipes and strums a guitar
but no longer sings madrigals due to catarrh.

Pete's flown to the Falklands – of course he flew solo –
to teach all the islanders how to play polo:
a charity chukka, in Peter's opinion,
calms their unease about ploys Argentinian

and socially, polo's become quite a pivot
– dodging old land-mines while treading down divots.
Pete has no ulterior motive – *of course* –
but is there a sponsor to buy him a horse?

Jane – such a trend-setter – still causes a ripple
with twenty-five curtain rings pierced through her nipple.
And Nigel's engaged! They all felt a thrill
when he made his commitment, in Balham, to Bill.

As for the "oldies", they're both keeping fit
chairing committees and doing their bit:
Roz reads the glossies to check out who's 'in'
and John's been created a Master of Spin,

they send us all greetings for freedom from stress
and hope we've experienced equal success.
Though life for the Borehams gets better and better
– at least we've a year before their next letter!

White…

No premonition. Never any warning -
only the thrill if you should sight one
stepping out from hoarfrost trees
and secretive, drifting mist...white.

Moon-flower white; *magnolia stellata;*
feathers of swans; seduction of untracked snow,
the emptiness of an unwritten page…
white is their perfect camouflage.

They are rarely encountered
and have no predictable habitat
– it's no good building a hide and lying in wait
and they never leave footprints -

but sometime, when you least expect it,
one may come trotting out of the mystery
fizzing like a sparkler
to dazzle you with possibilities.

Then beware! For they are never tame:
once you have seen one
you will be changed for ever
left unsatisfied … restless … searching ...

Red Kite

For George and Patricia

In my childhood it was often neglected,
waiting for windy days or expeditions to the sea
– dependent on us to remember its existence
before it could master the sky and stream away.

Even when released, it was an uncertain performer,
bumping grumpily along the ground, refusing
to become airborne; not trusting its scarlet sails
to the initiative of wind or enticement from branches.

Under the stairs, tail tangled in old tennis nets,
it slumped and slept with rusty croquet hoops,
cricket stumps and those midnight monsters
that inhabit dark cupboards at night.

Fifty years on, it has metamorphosed, acquired a mate,
been granted afresh freedom of Yorkshire air –
forked tail an instrument of delicate precision,
fanning and closing to balance helicopter-hover

above Wharfedale woods. Once it was refuse-collector
for mediaeval cities, today it soars over my fields
searching for carrion – but capable of killing too.
I flinch for my smallest dog as it dives in our direction

with flash of amber lights, sharpening its angled wings
on whetstone air, then up, away – one vole the less.
Once, from the top of a tall house, I saw a bird's-eye view
of conker-shiny back, polished like well-oiled saddlery.

Now, freed from dark oblivion, the Red Kite
builds again in Britain: *Look to lesser linen*
Shakespeare warns, when it hunts for bargain bedding
and renovates the tenements of crows.

Sighting a Kingfisher

A longed-for but elusive sight:
I watched a poem spear up-stream
as startling as a meteorite.

With opal feathers honed for flight
– like inspiration's piercing beams –
this longed for but elusive sight

of blue-winged stanzas flashed as bright
as psychedelic waking-dreams
of unexpected meteorites.

Ideas shot past me, spiked with light
– a glimse of form and rhyming scheme –
a longed for, but elusive sight.

It skimmed so close to water's night,
with navigating skill supreme,
shy bird-of-verse, rare meteorite,

I dared to hope it might alight
to lend me its poetic theme:
A longed for but elusive sight,
but transient – like a meteorite.